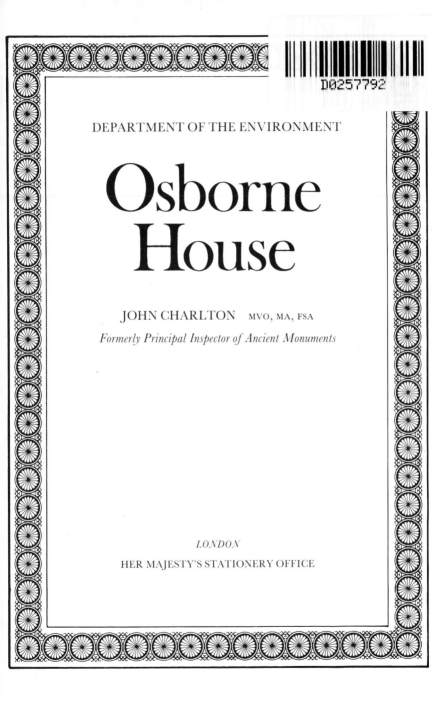

DEPARTMENT OF THE ENVIRONMENT

Osborne House

JOHN CHARLTON   MVO, MA, FSA

Formerly Principal Inspector of Ancient Monuments

LONDON

HER MAJESTY'S STATIONERY OFFICE

The paintings on pages 12 and 14–15 are reproduced by gracious permission of Her Majesty Queen Elizabeth II

ISBN 0 11 670069 6

Osborne House from the air

WHEN Queen Victoria married Prince Albert of Saxe-Coburg in 1840, she had three large houses to live in: Windsor Castle, Buckingham Palace and the Royal Pavilion at Brighton. These palaces, though well enough adapted for Court ceremonial, soon proved, to the parents of a growing family, to be unsuitable even for the small amount of private life allowed to royalty. Windsor had rooms for the young children and their nurses, but had no private gardens; Buckingham Palace had private gardens, but the nurseries had to be housed in the attics; Brighton Pavilion had neither nurseries nor gardens and was, moreover, in the middle of the town. So the Queen and her Consort felt the need for a family residence in the country. They wanted, to use the Queen's own words, 'a place of one's own, quiet and retired.' The Queen knew and liked the Isle of Wight. She had visited it twice as a girl, in 1831, when she laid the foundation stone of East Cowes Church, and again in 1833. Her inquiries, sympathetically promoted by Sir Robert Peel, then Prime Minister, led her to Osborne. Its situation, though relatively convenient to London, was yet secluded. Nearby was the sea, with a private beach for bathing and boating. After a trial visit the Queen wrote: 'It is

Main entrance to Pavilion, with Household wing on right

impossible to imagine a prettier spot—we have a charming beach quite to ourselves—we can walk anywhere without being followed or mobbed.' She was determined to purchase and in 1845 bought Osborne House with an estate of some 1000 acres (400ha) from Lady Isabella Blachford.

The existing house, however, was too small, and it was demolished to make room for the present mansion. This was designed by Prince Albert himself with the practical advice of Thomas Cubitt, the famous London builder, who actually prepared the drawings and executed the work. The Prince, who greatly admired the art and architecture of Italy, saw in the view over the Solent a resemblance to the Bay of Naples, and his design is a version of an Italian villa, with tall towers or campaniles and a first-floor balcony or loggia. Stepping down towards the sea are terrace-gardens adorned with fountains and statues in the Renaissance manner. The general style of residence and gardens incidentally set a new fashion so that soon many loyal subjects were building villas in the style of Her Majesty's Marine Residence at Osborne. The choice of builder may have quickened the spread of the Osborne style, for Thomas Cubitt was one of the first big building contractors (in the modern sense of the word) and built not merely streets, but entire suburbs. He was, incidentally, greatly interested in the latest

Marble figures and elaborate tiled floors are features of the corridors

building techniques, and made a study of the use of cast-iron beams. These were used in the building of Osborne, probably at his suggestion, for it was intended that the house should be fire-proof. On the interior decoration and the garden layout the Prince consulted his artistic adviser, Lewis Gruner.

On 23 June 1845, the Queen and her husband laid the first stone of the Pavilion Wing which they were themselves to occupy. It was completed in about a year and they went into residence in September 1846. The additional accommodation for guests and Household (the two eastern wings) was not, however, finished until 1851.

Except for their Highland holidays at Balmoral, the Queen and Prince Albert spent at Osborne all the time they could spare from their State duties; but their happy life together was suddenly cut short by the death of the Prince in 1861.

Marble bust of the Duchess of Kent, mother of
Queen Victoria, in arched recess in East Corridor

Queen Victoria's Sitting-room

Osborne House from the east

The Italian Garden

Significantly it was to Osborne that the heart-broken Queen retired after the Prince's death at Windsor, returning to the country home which was largely his creation and which reminded her of him at every turn. Throughout her forty years of widowhood, she endeavoured to keep every possible feature of house and grounds unaltered, as being sacred to his memory, and it was at Osborne, surrounded by relics of the husband whom she had loved and admired, that she died in 1901.

Since her death her wishes have been respected as far as possible, and the rooms where the Queen and the Prince lived and the gardens where they walked with their children are little changed from what they were at the time of the Prince's death.

King Edward VII, who already had Sandringham in Norfolk, did not wish to live at Osborne and presented most of the estate, which was the Queen's private property, to the nation. In 1904 the State Apartments, Swiss Cottage and part of the gardens (but not Queen Victoria's Private Suite) were opened to the public. In accordance with King Edward's wishes the eastern wings were made into a

The billiard-table with painted decorations designed by Prince Albert

The Royal Dining-room. On the far wall a picture after the famous one by Winterhalter shows Queen Victoria, Prince Albert and their children. Below is the solid mahogany sideboard and mahogany wine-cooler typical of the period. On the left is a copy of Winterhalter's portrait of Queen Victoria's mother, the Duchess of Kent

Convalescent Home for Officers. In 1954 Queen Elizabeth graciously granted permission for the Private Suite of her great-great-grandmother to be opened for public inspection.

The main part of the house is built round an open courtyard facing the drive. The Middle block, called the Pavilion Wing, was the first to be built. The ground floor contains the principal suite: Dining-room, Drawing-room and Billiard-room; on the first floor were the Private Apartments of the Queen and Prince Albert; on the top floor were formerly the Royal nurseries. On the right (east) side of the courtyard stand the Household Apartments, now part of the Convalescent Home and not open to the public. The low two-storeyed block to the left (west) side contains the later Durbar Room.

These three blocks and wings are joined together by the Grand Corridor which runs right round the courtyard—a convenient arrangement, and one in keeping with the Italianate character of the building. On the east side of the courtyard this corridor is open at first-floor level also in the manner of an Italian loggia.

Fireplace in the Queen's Drawing-room flanked by pedestal vases of hollow glass

Vase presented to Queen Victoria by Tsar Nicholas I of Russia

Prominent features are the two 'campaniles': the Flag Tower (107ft/32.6m) and the Clock Tower (90ft/27.4m). The clock itself was built for King George III in 1777 for use at Kew, and had originally only one dial, but was turned into a four-dial clock by the addition of mechanism taken from the clock removed from Brighton Pavilion in 1849.

The public entrance to the house is at present by way of the Durbar Room. The site of the Durbar Room was formerly a lawn on which, in the early days of Osborne, a marquee was erected for such receptions as were too large to be held in the State Apartments. When in 1890 this inconvenient arrangement was replaced by the present large hall, the Indian style was chosen for the interior in honour of the Queen's possessions in India, of which she had been declared Empress in 1876 and in which she felt great pride and interest.

The work was executed under the immediate direction of Bhai Ram Singh, an expert in Indian decorative techniques, whose portrait by Rudolph Swoboda appears at the entrance to the room. The father of Rudyard Kipling, John Lockwood Kipling, who for many years worked in the Indian Educational Service and was curator of Lahore Central Museum, may have been consulted

Painting by Landseer in 1866 of Queen Victoria at Osborne. The Queen reads dispatches from the box seen lying on the ground. At the horse's head is her Highlander attendant, John Brown, while her terrier Prince gazes up. On the seat are her daughters Princess Helena and Princess Alice

Prince Albert's writing desk

Sticks and umbrellas used
by Prince Albert

initially on its design. Above a teak dado, the wall and ceilings alike are intricately decorated in plaster. The tall chimneypiece has a plaster peacock displayed on its overmantel and is flanked by small oriels containing seated figures of Buddha. At the north end of the room is a wide service passage, over which is a triple-arched balcony, flanked by oriels.

When the Durbar Room was built, opportunity was taken to provide a first-floor suite of rooms; these were used by Princess Beatrice and her family. The Durbar Room now contains many Indian pieces, particularly ceremonial addresses and other items commemorative of the Jubilees of 1887 and 1897.

From the Durbar Room the State and Household Apartments are reached by means of the Grand Corridor. Its walls, and those of its lobbies, are lined with statues, pictures and cabinets, some of the last-named containing gifts presented to members of the Royal Family at various times. The stretch of corridor next to the Durbar Room is devoted mainly to Indian subjects, including portraits of the Queen's Indian servants who attended her in her later years. At the turn of the

Queen Victoria with her family and relatives at Windsor in 1887

From a painting by Laurits Tuxen in the Royal Collection

15

corridor are portraits of the Maharajah Duleep Singh and the Princess Gorumma by Winterhalter. Near the end of the corridor, on the left, is the Queen's lift. Near the fireplace beyond are some pictures of the earlier Osborne House, built by the Blachford family.

The short corridor now entered is called the Horn Corridor, from the Horn Room which may be seen on the left through a glass door. Nearly all its furniture is made of the antlers of deer, even the table tops being inlaid with sections of deer-horn. On the walls are pictures of some of the Queen's favourite horses and dogs.

The main living-rooms of the Royal Family open out of the Grand Corridor and consist of the Billiard-, Drawing- and Dining-rooms, arranged as a suite. The first, the Billiard-room, is structurally part of the Drawing-room, but, being out of sight of the latter, provided a place where the gentlemen of the Household could sit (on the raised leather seats opposite the billiard-table) though they were still theoretically in the Queen's presence. The Prince Consort, who was very fond of billiards, designed the elaborate painted decoration of the billiard-table, which was made by Magnus and partly garnished by Thurston. In front of the windows is an enormous porcelain vase, given to the Queen by Tsar Nicholas I on his visit to England in 1844, and painted with the views of his palace at St Petersburg. At the junction of the Billiard-room and Drawing-room is a rosewood cabinet decorated with porcelain plaques of Queen Victoria's children.

The Drawing-room is separated from the Billiard-room by a screen of imitation marble columns, but the decorative scheme is the same. The fireplace is of white marble with a richly gilded mirror over it. An unusual item of furniture is the grand piano (by Erard) with ormolu mounts and plaques of coloured porcelain. The latter, which are matched on the six cabinets in the room, bear representations of famous Italian paintings. The main suite of furniture is carved and gilt, with golden damask upholstery. Set about the room are life-size marble statues by Mary Thornycroft of the Royal children in the characters of Peace, Plenty, the Seasons, etc. One of the tables was given to the Queen by Pope Pius IX in 1859; its top is decorated with views of Rome.

The Dining-room has similar decorative treatment to the preceding rooms. Against the end wall stands a large sideboard which at Christmas used to bear a boar's head. In front of it are the dining-chairs used by the Royal children. Among the pictures are one of Queen Victoria, Prince Albert, and their family and another of the Duchess of Kent, the Queen's mother, both after Winterhalter. There is also a portrait group of the Prince and Princess of Wales (later King Edward VII and Queen Alexandra). It was in this room that the Queen's body lay in state before being taken to Windsor—an event commemorated by a brass plate in the floor.

The Dining-room gives on to the main staircase-hall, which contains a white marble group *The Amazons and the Argonaut* by J Engel and a posthumous bust of the Prince Consort by William Theed, dated Osborne, 1862. Above the stairs, which lead to the Private Apartments, is a large mural painting in fresco by Dyce, *Neptune entrusting the Command of the Sea to Britannia*. At the head of the stairs, a wide delicately ornamented archway leads to an alcove, which was formerly the pages' waiting-room. It contains a large naval portrait of Kaiser Wilhelm II (Queen Victoria's grandson), dated 1891. The small room between the alcove and the Queen's private apartments was a page's bedroom.

THE QUEEN'S PRIVATE SUITE

After the death of Prince Albert in 1861, the private suite was kept by the widowed Queen Victoria as far as possible as it was in his lifetime, and everything he used at Osborne lies where he left it. Throughout the suite (apart from his Dressing-room) many of the pictures are of his choosing.

Marble replicas of the limbs of the royal children

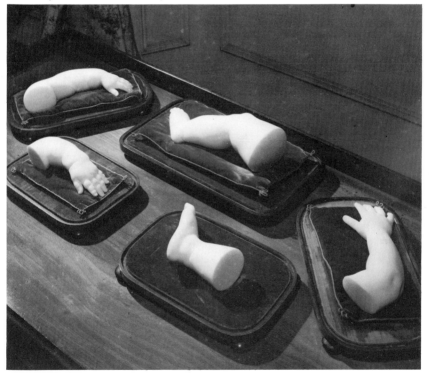

The suite consists of a Sitting-room, Bedroom and two Dressing-rooms with bathing closets, all commanding superb views of Osborne Bay and the Solent beyond. The first entered is the Prince's bathroom, on the walls of which are various pictures painted by the Prince himself, and some very early photographs of tableaux acted by the royal children. Next comes his Dressing- and Writing-room, which contains the table where he kept his papers, and upon it, among other things, his dispatch-box as a member of the Fine Arts Commission, of which he was the first chairman. In one window is his writing-desk and writing materials. Nearby are models in marble, probably by Mary Thornycroft, of the limbs of the royal infants, and of a hand of Queen Victoria carved in 1843. There also still remains, as he left it, his umbrella stand with umbrellas and walking sticks of various kinds used by him. There are also two pictures by the Queen of the royal children taking part in plays, one being Racine's *Athalie*, in which the Princess Royal played the part of Athalie and the Prince of Wales that of Abner.

Next to this room is the Queen's sitting-room, a large, square apartment having a wide curving bay with three tall windows. Outside is a balcony, shaded

Piano in the Queen's Sitting-room. Beyond is a German musical-box in the shape of a fort

The Sitting-room window. The view from
this window is shown on page 20

by a striped awning, where the Queen and the Prince often stood on summer
evenings to hear the song of the nightingales. The homely interior with its
patterned chintz upholstery, crowded with furniture and bric-à-brac of every
description, is typical of thousands of similar rooms of late Victorian England.

On the right of the doorway from Prince Albert's Dressing-room is a plaster
statuette group of the Queen, a spinning wheel and a favourite dog, Sharp. The
actual spinning wheel stands in one of the windows and there is a bronze statuette
of Sharp on the mantle-shelf of this room, as well as a life-size portrait of him by

C Burton Barber in the Queen's Dressing-room. The group of little chairs is from the nursery floor above, where they were used by Queen Victoria's children. The chair-covers were embroidered by the Duchess of Gloucester, the Queen's aunt.

Near the fireplace (where only beech logs were burnt) stand two brass-edged tables, to one of which are attached three bell-pulls for summoning the royal attendants. It was at these tables that the Queen wrote her letters and studied the contents of the Government dispatch-boxes which even at Osborne she did not neglect. Prince Albert sat at the left-hand table when submitting memoranda for the Queen's inspection. On and around the two tables are many portraits of her family and friends. In addition to that of Prince Albert, on a stand, there are several of the Prince and Princess of Wales (later King Edward VII and Queen Alexandra—one of 1874, in a forget-me-not frame, with a childhood portrait of the future King George V); one of Princess Alice (1843–78), great-grandmother of the present Duke of Edinburgh; and one, signed and dated 1898, of Princess Victoria, who was Princess Royal and mother of Kaiser Wilhelm II. Against one of the walls stands her baby-grand piano and near it is a typical German musical-box which plays a march from Wagner's *Tannhäuser*.

The Terrace Gardens, looking towards the sea

The Durbar Room

The State Drawing-room

The Swiss Cottage

Kitchen used by the royal children

Miniature grocer's shop

Queen Victoria's bathing-machine

The Queen's Dressing-room contains, in front of the window, her dressing-table with a mirror and toilet articles of Minton china. Opposite is her bath. It is flanked by portraits of Highland children painted by her at Balmoral in 1852.

The bedroom is simply but solidly furnished with tall mahogany wardrobes and a large square bed. At its foot is a comfortable sofa covered with patterned chintz. At its head is a large bronze memorial tablet inserted by her children. It was in this room, surrounded by her family, that she died on 22 January 1901. There is a picture by von Herkomer of the Queen on her death-bed to the left of the fireplace.

The corridor between the pavilion vestibule and the exit is paved with elaborate designs in encaustic tiles and they, like the general scheme of decoration, were inspired by the Prince Consort. To him also are due the plaster reliefs which copy, on a much reduced scale, famous classical friezes, like that of the Parthenon at Athens. Opposite the exit for the public is a niche containing a statue of Queen Victoria by John Gibson RA.

THE GROUNDS

The Prince had always taken an interest in forestry and gardening, but at Windsor Castle and Buckingham Palace he had not been able to indulge it, partly because the opportunities were limited and partly because the grounds and parks were under the control of the Office of Woods. Osborne was, however, the private property of the Queen and she had virtually a free hand. In much of the area, assisted by Mr Toward, who was steward at Osborne for many years, he planted thousands of traditional English trees—oak, elm and beech. Nearer the house, however, he planted foreign trees, mainly evergreens or conifers.

THE SWISS COTTAGE

The Cottage stands about half a mile east of the house and is reached by a tree-lined avenue called High Walk. It was brought in sections from Switzerland and erected in 1853–54. It was then handed over to the royal children as a place where the princes could learn carpentry and gardening and their sisters the rudiments of housekeeping and cookery. There they often entertained their parents to tea. Their garden tools and wheelbarrows (each marked with the owner's initials) may be seen in a thatched shed close at hand. Nearby is Queen

Queen Victoria's Bedroom

Victoria's bathing-machine, which used to be lowered down a sloping pier in Osborne Bay. After she first used the machine on 30 July 1874, she made the following entry in her diary:

Drove down to the beach with my maids and went into the bathing machine, where I undressed and bathed in the sea (for the first time in my life), a very nice bathing woman attending me. I thought it delightful till I put my head under the water, when I thought I should be stifled. After dressing again, drove back.

Behind the cottage is a miniature fortress with tiny brick barracks, earthwork fortifications and wooden cannon. Built in 1860 by the ten-year-old Prince Arthur, later Field Marshal the Duke of Connaught, it was long the playground of the royal children.

The cottage itself is a typical wooden Swiss chalet. Round the outside are carved proverbs and quotations from the Psalms in German. The first room entered on the first floor was the general Sitting-room or Parlour, used principally by the children and grand-children of Queen Victoria. In a cabinet between the windows is a collection of porcelain miniature objects which Queen Victoria formed when a child at Kensington Palace. The Dressing-room of the Cottage was used by Queen Victoria, the Prince Consort and their children. The furniture and fittings are now set out as they were in 1854. Next comes the Dining-room, its furniture and ornaments collected by the Prince in Switzerland. The arrangement of this room has not been disturbed since it was first used in 1854. An interesting exhibit is the writing-table used by Queen Victoria, exactly as she left it. On the ground floor are the two small kitchens with miniature charcoal ranges and cooking implements, made specially for the royal children.

Dining-room in the Swiss Cottage with its small-scale furniture

The royal children's gardening tools, each with its owner's initials

THE SWISS COTTAGE MUSEUM

The second building, the Swiss Cottage Museum, originally housed the many curiosities, botanical and otherwise, collected by the royal children on their father's instructions. It was completed in 1862. The whole collection was carefully rearranged and classified in 1915, and the various exhibits are now placed under distinctive headings.

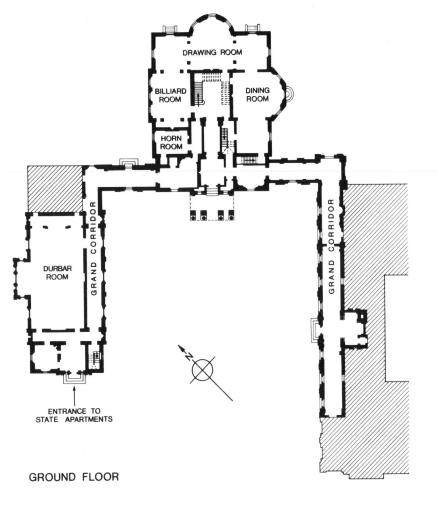

DRAWING ROOM

BILLIARD
ROOM

DINING
ROOM

HORN
ROOM

DURBAR
ROOM

GRAND CORRIDOR

GRAND CORRIDOR

N

ENTRANCE TO
STATE APARTMENTS

GROUND FLOOR

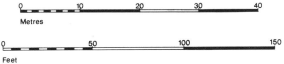

| 0 | 10 | 20 | 30 | 40 |
Metres

| 0 | 50 | 100 | 150 |
Feet

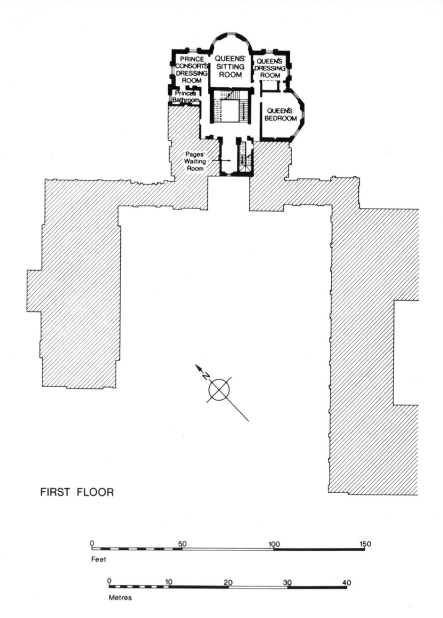

FIRST FLOOR

PRINCE CONSORT'S DRESSING ROOM

QUEENS' SITTING ROOM

QUEEN'S DRESSING ROOM

Prince's Bathroom

QUEEN'S BEDROOM

Pages' Waiting Room

Feet
0 50 100 150

Metres
0 10 20 30 40

Printed in England for Her Majesty's Stationery Office
by Willsons Printers (Leicester) Limited
Dd 698658 K965 1/81